Doomed to Disappear
Endangered Species

by Kathy Kinsner

TABLE OF CONTENTS

Introduction

Many **species,** or kinds, of animals that inhabit Earth are in danger of vanishing forever. These species are described as **endangered**. Some experts think that we may be losing as many as 30,000 species each year!

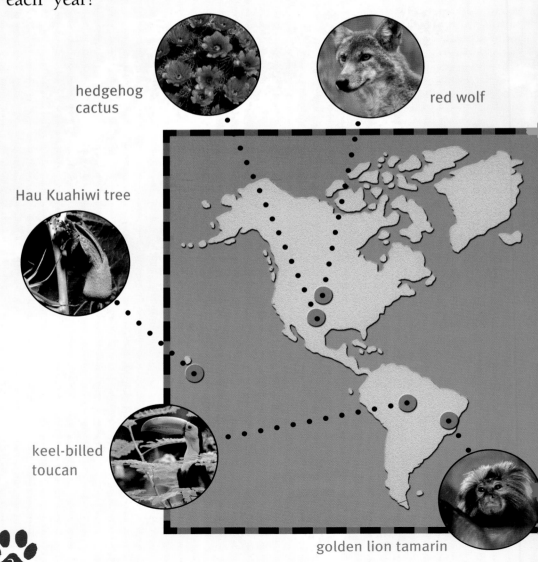

hedgehog cactus

red wolf

Hau Kuahiwi tree

keel-billed toucan

golden lion tamarin

Scientists think that at least 10 million species exist on Earth today. These species include every kind of animal—from giant whales and elephants to creatures too small to see without a microscope. They also include every kind of plant—from trees that tower high above to plants at the bottom of the sea.

When the last plant or animal of its kind dies, the species is **extinct**. Scientists work hard to figure out which species might be struggling to survive. Endangered species are close to becoming extinct. **Threatened** species are close to becoming endangered.

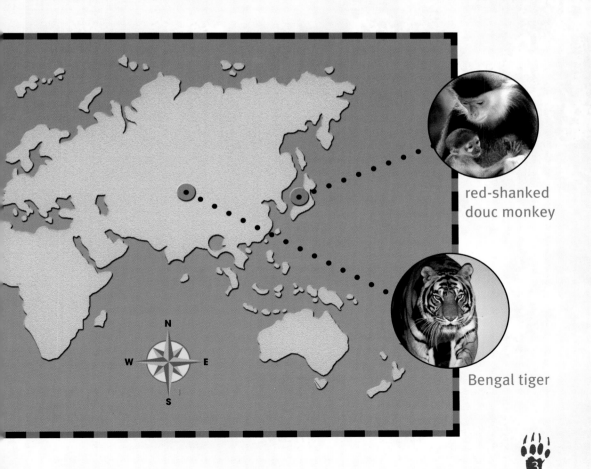

red-shanked douc monkey

Bengal tiger

We're All Connected

The loss of a keystone species—such as the sea otter—can cause great changes in its ecosystem. Oil spills, the fishing industry, and pollution are all possible threats to sea otters.

Sea otters eat animals called sea urchins. When there are fewer sea otters, fewer sea urchins are eaten. The sea urchin population increases.

Sea urchins eat kelp, a kind of seaweed. As the population of sea urchins increases, more kelp is eaten.

In the past, people often focused on one endangered species at a time. They did not realize that what happened to one species affected other species, too. Often these effects did not show up for years and years.

Then people started thinking about how a species is connected to other species. They thought about how each species fits into the **ecosystem** where it lives.

The life of the southern sea otter, a threatened species, provides a good illustration of how this connectedness works. The sea otter plays a very important role in its ecosystem. For this reason, it is called a **keystone species**.

Without the plants, the fish no longer have a place to hide. They are clearly visible to their enemies.

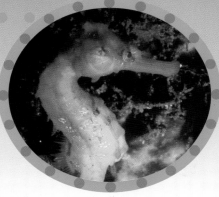

The kelp begins to disappear. Kelp plays its own important role in the ecosystem. The plants provide hiding places for tiny fish.

Southern sea otters live in the Pacific Ocean, off the coast of California. Scientists estimate that 250 years ago there were 16,000 to 20,000 sea otters living there.

Sea otter fur is beautiful. So people hunted and killed sea otters to provide fur for clothing. The hunting continued for more than 150 years. By the early 1900s, sea otters had nearly disappeared from the California coastline.

People in California passed laws to protect the sea otters, and soon the sea otter population began to increase. But in the 1970s, the sea otter population again declined. This time, oil spills were to blame.

In 1977, the southern sea otter was listed as a threatened species by the United States Fish and Wildlife Service. By the 1990s, more than 2,000 sea otters were living off the coast of California. While this increase in the number is good, it is still too small to ensure the survival of the species.

Oil spills such as this one in the Pacific Ocean off the coast of South America pose a threat to animal survival.

IT'S A FACT

Figuring out how to save an endangered species is tricky, and sometimes even good ideas don't work! Because southern sea otters live in a small area of the Pacific Ocean, a disease could wipe out the otters forever. Scientists hoped to solve this problem by starting a new colony of sea otters. For three years, scientists trapped sea otters and moved them to an island off the California coast. But the sea otters didn't take to their new home. The colony dwindled in size. Some otters returned to their original home. Most just disappeared.

What We've Lost

In 1884, the famous naturalist and artist John James Audubon wrote:

"I...began to mark with my pencil, making a dot for every flock that passed...As the birds poured in in countless multitudes, I rose, and counting the dots then put down, found that 163 had been made in twenty-one minutes."

Extinction is a natural part of Earth's history. In fact, about 95 percent of all the living things that have existed on Earth are now extinct. However, the rate of extinction has increased dramatically in the last 300 years. Human actions have contributed significantly to this situation.

Passenger Pigeon

Billions of passenger pigeons lived in North America when the first Europeans arrived. There were so many of these birds that a single flock sometimes took hours to pass overhead.

As more people arrived, more forests were cut and more land was plowed. The passenger pigeons had smaller and smaller areas in which to nest and find food. Farmers were shooting the pigeons to protect their crops.

Hunters began killing large numbers of passenger pigeons and selling them as food. The pigeons were shot, knocked to the ground with sticks, and smoked out of trees. Because so many birds gathered in each tree, trapping them with nets was easy.

In the late 1800s, some people tried to make killing passenger pigeons illegal. Unfortunately, they were too late. In 1914, the last passenger pigeon, a bird named Martha, died in a zoo in Cincinnati, Ohio. A species whose numbers had once been in the billions was gone forever.

Passenger pigeons will never be seen again.

Miss Waldron's red colobus monkey is almost certainly extinct.

Miss Waldron's Red Colobus Monkey

Hunting is not the only cause of extinction. It's not even the most important cause. Loss of **habitat**—the place where a species lives—is an even greater problem.

In 1933, a species of monkey was discovered in an African rain forest. It was named in honor of Miss F. Waldron, who was traveling with the person who first recognized this as a "new" kind of monkey.

Soon people began coming to the rain forest in search of diamonds. They cut trees and built roads. They cleared land for farming. As a result, the monkeys' habitat became smaller and smaller.

Not one Miss Waldron's monkey has been seen for over 25 years. Between 1993 and 1999, scientists searched for the monkeys in the rain forest where they once lived. The scientists found no monkeys of that kind. Instead, they found evidence that hunters had gotten to the monkeys before the scientists could.

If no members of a species are seen for 50 years, the species is officially extinct. This determination is made by organizations such as the World Conservation Union (IUCN after its original name—International Union for Conservation of Nature and Natural Resources). Scientists don't expect to find any more Miss Waldron's red colobus monkeys. So in 2000, they declared that the species is probably extinct.

As more and more rain forests are cut for wood and cleared for farming, animals have less and less living space.

Monteverde Golden Toad

Sometimes scientists cannot determine the exact cause of a species' decline. This is the case of the Monteverde golden toad.

These toads lived in just one place on Earth—the cloud forest of Costa Rica. Not much was known about the golden toads. They appeared in huge numbers during the rainy season. After they mated and laid their eggs, they disappeared into the forest until the next rainy season.

In 1987, there were lots of golden toads in the cloud forest. By 1988, they were almost gone. The last one was seen in 1989.

Why did this species disappear so quickly? Nobody knows for sure. Scientists think that one or two dry years made the toads too weak to fight disease.

Monteverde golden toads

✔ POINT

Read More About It

Using reference materials, identify the weather patterns in Costa Rica from 1986 to 1990. Draw a conclusion about your findings.

IT'S A FACT

The kakapo is a parrot that cannot fly. It lives in New Zealand, an island country. For years, only one kind of animal hunted the kakapo—the eagle. To protect itself, the kakapo just stood still. It blended into its surroundings, and an eagle couldn't see it.

Everything changed when people came to New Zealand. They brought cats, dogs, ferrets, and rats with them, and those animals ate the kakapos. Standing still was no protection at all.

Today, only 124 kakapos are left in the world. To protect them, people moved them to small islands where they are safe. When the kakapos lay their eggs, volunteers take care of the eggs to make sure that they hatch.

A Success Story

When scientists count birds, they often talk about the number of pairs rather than the number of birds. Here's why: Imagine trying to count birds as they fly from one tree to another! It's difficult, so scientists often count nests instead. That's easier and more accurate, because the nests don't move around. Each nest represents a pair of birds, one male bird and one female bird.

The peregrine (PAIR-eh-grin) falcon is one of the fastest birds on Earth. Falcons dive at more than 180 miles per hour.

Peregrine falcons are **birds of prey**. That is, they eat other animals. They can snatch their meal right out of the sky. Adult peregrines have few natural enemies. People present the biggest danger to these birds.

About 60 years ago, there were nearly 350 pairs of peregrine falcons east of the Mississippi River. By 1965, there were none.

What caused the disappearance of peregrine falcons? Scientists discovered that it was DDT, a chemical used to kill insects on crops and trees. Small birds ate insects that had been poisoned by DDT. Then the falcons ate the small birds. The DDT built up in the falcons' bodies and affected their eggs. The eggs had weak shells. Many never hatched. Fewer and fewer baby falcons were born.

In 1970, scientists began a program to help the peregrine falcon. They removed eggs from the falcons' nests and took them to a laboratory to hatch. Once the baby birds hatched, scientists put them into a nest where they could be fed by adult falcons. The adult birds took care of the babies as if they were their own.

This scientist feeds young falcons.

A falcon puppet hides the human hand that feeds the chicks.

To survive in the wild, the young birds would have to be able to hunt for food. Just before the birds were old enough to fly, they were moved to a box high above the ground. Each day, scientists dropped food into the box, just as the birds' parents would do.

Soon the young peregrine falcons tried their wings. As they became stronger fliers, the birds spent more and more time hunting for food. After about seven weeks, the young falcons were ready to live on their own.

Scientists repeated this process in other parts of the country. However, the real test came in the years that followed. Would the peregrine falcons raised in **captivity** survive in the wild?

The answer was yes. More than 30 years later, about 1,650 pairs of peregrine falcons live in the United States. In 1998, the United States Fish and Wildlife Service took the peregrine falcon off the endangered species list.

IT'S A FACT

Where do peregrine falcons nest today? Amazingly, some live in cities! The falcon in this photo lives in San Francisco. They build their nests on ledges 50 to 200 feet off the ground. The bridges and skyscrapers of a city seem like perfect places to watch for passing birds that might make a good meal.

Other Success Stories

SPECIES   **HABITAT**

AMERICAN BISON

the plains and prairies of North America

BLUE WHALE

the oceans of the world

GIANT PANDA

the bamboo forests of China

BALD EAGLE

the mountains, valleys, and forests of the United States and Canada

DESERT TORTOISE

the deserts of North America

THREATS

FUTURE

They were hunted for their hides and for sport. By 1890, there were only about 1,000 left.

The bison population has grown since conservation efforts began 100 years ago.

Huge numbers were killed for their meat and blubber. Pollution and fishing nets can also harm whales.

International laws have made hunting blue whales and buying or selling whale products illegal. However, some countries continue to hunt whales.

Destruction of the panda's habitat is the major threat. Illegal hunting is also a problem.

China no longer allows logging in most panda habitats.

The pesticide DDT caused eagles to lay eggs with thin shells. DDT is no longer used in the United States, but destruction of habitat still threatens them.

Programs to raise baby bald eagles in captivity and release them into the wild have been successful.

The biggest threat is human activity. Ranching, mining, and building destroy habitat. Off-road vehicles crush young tortoises.

Governments and private companies have worked together to set aside land where tortoises are protected.

Plant Life Can Be Endangered, Too

Endangered plants don't get as much publicity as endangered animals, but they are just as important. Plants provide food, hold soil in place, and make the oxygen we breathe. Plants are also the source of some medicines.

Florida Scrub Mint

The Florida scrub mint is an endangered species found in central Florida. It has lost its habitat to public use. Scientists studying this plant noticed that there were no insects on it. They suspected that its minty smell might be a natural insect repellent. Their experiments proved them right. They're hopeful that farmers can use a chemical found in the scrub mint to keep insects away from crops.

Rosy Periwinkle

The rosy periwinkle grows in the rain forest of Madagascar—an enormous island east of Africa. The periwinkle grows only one foot high, but this is one powerful plant! Several medicines have come from it. One of them helps people who suffer from certain kinds of leukemia, a blood disease. The periwinkle is not endangered right now, but the rain forest where it grows is disappearing quickly. So this plant must now be **cultivated**.

The biggest threat to the rosy periwinkle in nature is the growing human population of Madagascar. More people need more food, so they cut and burn rain forests to make room for farms. Once a tropical rain forest is gone, there's no way to get it back. Who knows what other important plants may never be discovered?

✔ POINT
Think It Over
Which do you think is more important: human living conditions or medical advancements?

Tropical Rain Forest

Tropical rain forests cover less than 10 percent of the world, but they contain more than half the world's plant and animal species. Located near the equator, tropical rain forests are hot year-round and get huge amounts of rain.

Within a rain forest are many habitats. Plants grow well here. The tallest trees are 200 feet high and hundreds of years old. There are so many trees that their leaves block the sunlight.

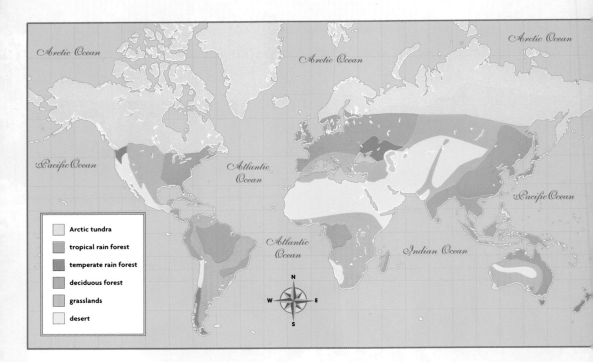

Arctic Ocean

Arctic Ocean

Arctic Ocean

Pacific Ocean

Atlantic Ocean

Pacific Ocean

Atlantic Ocean

Indian Ocean

- Arctic tundra
- tropical rain forest
- temperate rain forest
- deciduous forest
- grasslands
- desert

Tropical rain forests are located near the equator, where it's hot all year long.

The rain forest is home to an abundance of wildlife—colorful birds, huge snakes, gorillas, and elephants, to name a few.

Why do people destroy rain forests? Often, they don't think about the future. They just take what they need. Logging companies cut the best trees. Mining companies pollute the water supply. People grow crops.

Saving the rain forests means balancing what humans need today and what's good for Earth in the future. People are doing that in the Central African Republic, a country in Africa. Working with a conservation organization called the World Wildlife Fund, the government has set aside two wildlife **preserves** to make sure that this rain forest survives.

These students, atop the Lincoln Memorial in Washington, D.C., demonstrate for a good cause: Earth First!

IT'S A FACT

Katy Payne listens to elephants. She makes recordings of elephant sounds and observations of elephant behavior. When she's not in the rain forests of the Central African Republic, she's analyzing her data at Cornell University in New York. While Payne was studying elephants in Africa, she wrote letters home describing the sights and sounds of the rain forest.

April 30, 2000

It is our second night here; we arrived after ten hours of wild driving...Beyond us the night is full of insect calls...distant frogs, an owl, and beyond that a deep peaceful silence except for every now and then a distant elephant rumble or roar.

June 23, 2000

Things cool down after rain...The elephants stop competing (over space at the watering holes) and have fun. They slither and squirm, wallow, and rub themselves all over in mudholes, emerging terracotta (brownish-orange) or black or golden or bright orange depending on the clay pit visited.

25

Elephants are a keystone species in the rain forest of Africa. They are important to the survival of other animals—and of the rain forest itself.

Unfortunately, African elephants are in danger. From 1979 to 1989, half the elephants on the African continent disappeared. Many elephants were killed so that their tusks could be sold for products made of ivory. In 1989, elephants were put on an international endangered species list, and more than 115 countries agreed to make selling ivory a crime.

Elephants use their tusks to dig for salt and other minerals in the soil. This digging loosens the soil and allows rainwater to reach the roots of plants.

Conservation Efforts

People didn't give much thought to conservation until the 1900s. Before then, it was easy to suppose that an unlimited number of animals roamed the land. However, after hundreds of years of hunting and fishing, species that were once plentiful began to disappear. People began taking steps to protect wildlife.

In the United States, Congress passed a series of laws in the 1960s and 1970s to clean up the environment. The most famous of these laws was the Endangered Species Act. It protected endangered animals and plants.

In 1872, the United States Congress made the Yellowstone area in Wyoming a national park. This was the first national park. It was the beginning of an effort to preserve land in its natural state.

In 1973, people from 80 countries met to figure out how to work together to protect endangered species. The countries agreed on rules that would prevent people from selling or buying products made from endangered plants and animals. Today, 150 countries belong to this organization, known as CITES (Convention on International Trade in Endangered Species of Wild Fauna and Flora).

Another organization, the World Conservation Union, coordinates endangered species research in countries around the world. It publishes lists of all Earth's endangered species.

The government of Ecuador made the Galápagos Islands a national park in 1959.

What You Can Do

Endangered plants and animals need your help to survive.
You can make a difference!

Help preserve habitats. When you're in a natural habitat, stay on paths and trails. Leave all living things where you find them.

Use less. Shut lights, radio, and TV off when you leave a room. Ride your bike or walk instead of riding in a car.

Waste less. Buy products with less packaging. Save paper by using both sides, and recycle waste paper. Turn the water off while you brush your teeth or wash dishes.

Make your voice heard. Write letters to companies and government officials to let them know that protecting endangered species is important to you.

Read more about endangered species. Talk to your family and friends about what you've learned.

Quick Clicks

Check out these wild Web sites.

➤ **www.kidsplanet.org**
Defenders of Wildlife
Get the facts on many endangered species and great ideas for ways to help them.

➤ **www.ran.org**
Rainforest Action Network
Here you'll find lots of ideas for kids who want to get involved.

➤ **www.rainforest-alliance.org**
Rain Forest Alliance
Click on the Kids and Teachers section for tools that connect kids to conservation.

➤ **www.nwf.org/kids**
National Wildlife Federation's Kidzone
There's something interesting for everyone here.

➤ **www.rarespecies.org**
Rare Species Conservatory Foundation
"Learning Center" is perfect for animal-trivia fans.

➤ **www.worldwildlife.org**
World Wildlife Fund
Figure out how biodiversity helps Earth.

➤ **www.sandiegozoo.com**
San Diego Zoo
To see a day in the life of a panda, click on "Panda Cam."

✔ POINT
Read More About It
With a group member, choose one of the Web sites listed. Research the identified information.

Glossary

bird of prey | (BERD UV PRAY) a bird that hunts animals as food (page 14)

captivity | (kap-TIH-vih-tee) confinement in a nature preserve or zoo (page 17)

cultivated | (KUL-tih-vate-ed) grown in controlled conditions (page 21)

ecosystem | (EE-koh-sis-tem) living things, their environment, and their interaction (page 5)

endangered | (in-DANE-jerd) in danger of becoming extinct (page 2)

extinct | (ik-STINGKT) no longer in existence (page 3)

habitat | (HA-bih-tat) a place where a plant or animal naturally grows or lives (page 10)

keystone species | (KEE-stone SPEE-sheez) a species that other species depend on (page 5)

preserve | (prih-ZERV) a place set aside for the protection of wildlife (page 24)

species | (SPEE-sheez) a kind of plant or animal (page 2)

threatened | (THREH-tend) close to becoming endangered (page 3)

INDEX